A Note to Parents and Teachers

DK READERS is a compelling reading programme for children. The programme is designed in conjunction with leading literacy experts, including Cliff Moon M.Ed., who has spent many years as a teacher and teacher educator specializing in reading. Cliff Moon has written more than 160 books for children and teachers. He is series editor to Collins Big Cat.

Beautiful illustrations and superb full-colour photographs combine with engaging, easy-to-read stories to offer a fresh approach to each subject in the series. Each DK READER is guaranteed to capture a child's interest while developing his or her reading skills, general knowledge, and love of reading.

The five levels of DK READERS are aimed at different reading abilities, enabling you to choose the books that are exactly right for your child:

Pre-level 1: Learning to read
Level 1: Beginning to read
Level 2: Beginning to read alone
Level 3: Reading alone
Level 4: Proficient readers

The "normal" age at which a child begins to read can be anywhere from three to eight years old. Adult participation through the lower levels is very helpful for providing encouragement, discussing storylines and sounding out unfamiliar words.

No matter which level you select, you can be sure that you are helping your child lern to read, then read to learn!

LONDON, NEW YORK, MUNICH,
MELBOURNE, and DELHI

Series Editor Penny Smith
Art Editor Leah Germann
DTP Designer Almudena Díaz
Production Angela Graef
Picture Research Myriam Megharbi
Dinosaur Consultant Dougal Dixon

Reading Consultant
Cliff Moon, M.Ed.

Published in Great Britain by
Dorling Kindersley Limited
80 Strand, London WC2R 0RL

Copyright © 2006 Dorling Kindersley Limited, London
A Penguin Company
This edition, 2012

2 4 6 8 10 9 7 5 3
007-184578 -July 2012

A CIP catalogue record for this book
is available from the British Library

ISBN: 978-1-40937-367-4

Colour reproduction by Colourscan, Singapore
Printed and bound in China by L. Rex Printing Co. Ltd.

The publisher would like to thank the following for their kind permission
to reproduce their photographs:
a=above; c=centre; b=below; l=left; r=right; t=top; b/g=background

Alamy Images: Robert Harding Picture Library Ltd 20-21 b/g, 31cr b/g.
Corbis: Matt Brown 26-27 b/g; Larry Lee Photography 18-19 b/g, 30cl
b/g; W. Wayne Lockwood, MD 4-5c b/g, 8-9 b/g; Charles Mauzy 5tcl
b/g, 24-25 b/g; Craig Tuttle 4br b/g, 14-15 b/g, 16-17 b/g, 28-29 b/g,
31bcl b/g; Jim Zuckerman 6-7, 30cb b/g. **DK Images:** Jon Hughes
4-5c, 8-9. **Getty Images:** J.P. Nacivet 22-23 b/g, 31tr b/g;
James Randklev 4c b/g, 10-11 b/g.

All other images © Dorling Kindersley
For more information see: www.dkimages.com

Discover more at
www.dk.com

DK READERS

LEARNING
pre-level
1
TO READ

Meet the
Dinosaurs

A Dorling Kindersley Book

Watch out!
Here come
the dinosaurs.

Here is the scary Tyrannosaurus (tie-RAN-oh-SORE-us). It has sharp teeth.

Tyrannosaurus

teeth

Here is the huge
Brachiosaurus
(BRAK-ee-oh-SORE-us)
It has a long neck.

Brachiosaurus

neck

Here is the tough
Triceratops
(try-SER-uh-tops).
It has three horns.

Triceratops

horn

Here is the fierce
Velociraptor
(vell-OSS-ee-rap-tor).
It has sharp claws.

Velociraptor

claw

crest

Corythosaurus

Here is the noisy
Corythosaurus
(koe-rith-oh-SORE-us).
It has a bright crest.

Here is the small Compsognathus (komp-sog-NATH-us). It runs quickly.

foot

Compsognathus

Here is the clever
Troodon
(TROE-oh-don).
It has large eyes.

Troodon

eye

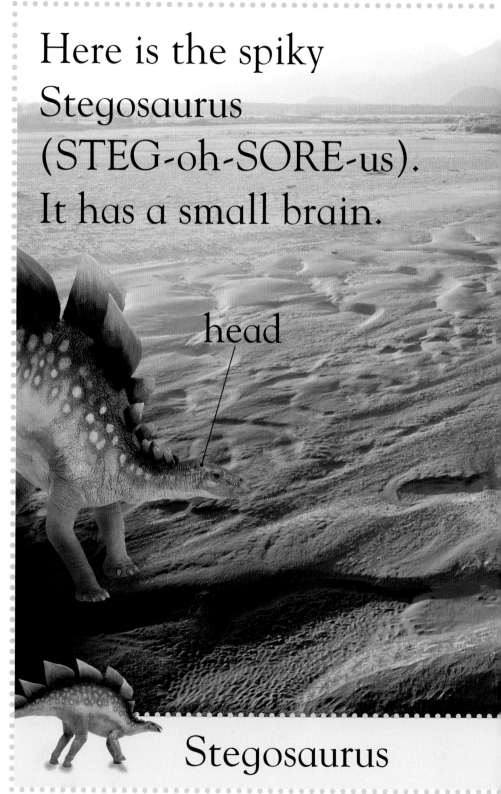

Here is the spiky
Stegosaurus
(STEG-oh-SORE-us).
It has a small brain.

head

Stegosaurus

Here is the bird-like
Gallimimus
(gal-lee-MEEM-us).
It has slim legs
and a beak.

leg

Gallimimus

beak

spike

Iguanodon

Here is the strong
Iguanodon
(ig-WAHN-oh-don).
It has a spike on
each thumb.

Here is the plant-eating Stegoceras (STEG-oh-SER-us). It has a thick skull.

skull

Stegoceras

Here is the armour-plated
Ankylosaurus
(an-KIE-luh-SORE-us).
It has a tail club.

Ankylosaurus

club

Which dinosaur
do you like best?
The one who is...

clever?   scary?

bird-like?

spiky?

noisy?

Glossary

Ankylosaurus
a plant-eating dinosaur with a tail-club

Brachiosaurus
a very tall plant-eating dinosaur

Triceratops
a plant-eating dinosaur with three horns

Tyrannosaurus
a large meat-eating dinosaur

Velociraptor
a fast and agile meat-eating dinosaur